Digital Transformation

Flourish amidst the Age of Extinction: "Master the Art of Survival!"

By

Jeff Harmon

**Copyright © by Jeff Harmon 2023.
All privileges preserved.**

Prior to duplicating or reproducing this document in any way, it is essential to obtain the publisher's authorization. As a result, the information contained herein cannot be electronically stored, transferred, or maintained in a database. Furthermore, the document may not be partially or wholly copied, scanned, faxed, or retained without explicit permission from the publisher or creator.

Digital Transformation

Table of contents

Introduction
Chapter One
What is digital transformation?
Chapter Two
What are the four main areas of digital?
Chapter Three
The rewards of digital transformation.
Chapter Four
Is digital transformation a good career?
Chapter Five
Does digital transformation needs coding?
Chapter Six
Which expertise is required for digital transformation?
Chapter Seven
What are the 3 R's of digital transformation?
Chapter Eight
What are the essential skills for digital transformation?

Introduction

The future is here, and innovation is king, with technology ruling supreme. Greetings from the age of digital transformation, a ground-breaking journey that is redefining business models, revolutionizing entire industries, and empowering people like never before. In this exhilarating era of limitless potential, we embrace the confluence of cutting-edge technology and human potential, propelling us toward unrivaled development, efficiency, and success. Prepare for an astonishing journey as we reveal the secrets of digital transformation and open up a world of

limitless possibilities. Do you have the capacity to alter reality? Get the copy now…

Chapter One

What is digital transformation?

The process of adopting digital technology to radically change the way businesses function and give value to their consumers is referred to as digital transformation.

It entails integrating digital technologies into all elements of a company's operations, such as its processes, systems, goods, services, and customer contacts.

Utilizing the power of technology to automate and streamline operations, improve operational efficiency, improve customer experience, and drive innovation is what digital transformation entails. It necessitates a mental and cultural shift, as well as investments in the appropriate infrastructure, skills, and resources.

Adopting cloud computing, implementing artificial intelligence and machine learning, developing mobile apps, exploiting big data analytics, and embracing the Internet of Things (IoT) are some examples of digital transformation activities.

The purpose of digital transformation is to enable businesses to become more agile, responsive, and customer-focused, as well as to drive growth and competitive advantage in a digitally-enhanced world.

The transition from a traditional brick-and-mortar store to an e-commerce website is a concrete illustration of digital transformation.
Consider a clothes retailer that decides to grow its business by opening an online store.
The company in this scenario is undertaking a digital transition by putting its operations online.

To Enhance customer interaction and revenues, this transition entails installing numerous technologies such as an e-commerce platform, digital marketing tools, and analytics software.

The company may provide its items to customers all over the world, create a more personalized shopping experience, and track customer behavior to improve its products and services by leveraging digital technologies. This change can assist the organization in boosting revenue, lowering costs, and competing more effectively in a more digital environment.

Digital Transformation

Chapter Two

What are the four main areas of digital?

Digital transformation can encompass a wide variety of changes, but the four main areas of digital transformation are typically identified as follows:

- **Customer Experience:** This involves improving how consumers interact with a business through digital

  channels. This could include constructing a user-friendly

  website, developing mobile applications, or implementing

chatbots to enhance customer service.

- **Operational Processes:** This involves automating or digitizing internal processes to enhance efficiency, productivity, and overall performance.

 This could include implementing new software and technologies, such as cloud computing, robotic process automation (RPA), or artificial intelligence (AI) systems.

- **Business Models:** This involves using digital technologies to create new products or services, or to transform the way the business operates. This could include adopting a subscription-based model, creating new revenue streams through data monetization, or implementing blockchain technology to enhance supply chain transparency.

- **Organizational Culture:** This involves nurturing a culture of innovation and digital transformation within the organization.

This could include investing in employee training and development,
fostering collaboration and experimentation, or establishing

new leadership roles to drive digital transformation initiatives.

Chapter Three

The rewards of digital transformation.

The benefit of digital change is to make your business more competitive. Additional perks include the following:

- **It engages customers by offering a better user experience:** Yes, improving the user experience is one of the key ways to engage people in the digital age. With

the rise of digital technologies and the growing reliance on

online channels, customers have come to expect seamless and personalized experiences across all touchpoints.

By offering a better user experience, businesses can enhance customer satisfaction and loyalty, increase conversion rates, and drive revenue growth.

There are many ways to improve the user experience, such as

designing user-friendly interfaces, providing personalized content and suggestions, offering fast and convenient checkout

processes, and ensuring that websites and applications are optimized for mobile devices.

Additionally, adopting chatbots, virtual assistants, and other AI-powered tools can help businesses provide faster and more efficient customer service, further enhancing the overall user experience.

- **It improves customer loyalty through engagement:** Improving the user experience is one of the key ways to engage customers in the digital age. With the rise of digital technologies and the growing reliance on online channels, customers have come to expect seamless and personalized experiences across all touchpoints.

By offering a better user experience, businesses can enhance customer satisfaction and loyalty, increase conversion rates, and drive revenue growth.

There are many ways to improve the user experience, such as designing user-friendly interfaces, providing personalized content and suggestions, offering fast and convenient checkout processes, and ensuring that

websites and applications are optimized for mobile devices. Additionally, adopting chatbots, virtual assistants, and other AI-powered tools can help businesses provide faster and more efficient customer service, further enhancing the overall user experience.

- **It motivates employees with improved tools for success:** Providing employees with improved tools for success can be a powerful motivator, as it shows that their employer values their contributions and wants to support their growth and development.

When employees have access to better tools, they can work more efficiently and effectively, which can improve their sense of accomplishment and satisfaction. Additionally, using new and improved tools can provide employees with a feeling of excitement and novelty in their work. They may feel more engaged and interested in their jobs when they have access to cutting-edge technology or innovative processes. However, it's important to remember that simply providing new tools is not enough to motivate employees.

It's crucial to also provide adequate training and support to ensure that employees know how to use the tools successfully.

Furthermore, workers may also require other forms of support, such as feedback and recognition, to feel
truly driven and engaged in their work.

- **It makes a group more efficient:** By adopting digital tools and processes, organizations can simplify routine tasks, streamline workflows, and reduce the time it takes to complete tasks.

This can lead to cost savings, better productivity, and faster time-to-market for new products or services. Digital transformation can also improve communication and collaboration within a company, as digital tools can enable teams to work together more effectively regardless of their location or time zone.

Additionally, digital transformation can help organizations to gain better insights into their operations and customers, allowing them to make data-driven choices and adapt quickly to changing market conditions.

However, it's worth noting that digital transformation is not a one-time event, but rather an ongoing process of continuous growth. Organizations need to be prepared to adapt to new technologies and to continue to invest in digital transformation to stay competitive in the long run.

- **It modernizes your IT infrastructure:** Digital transformation can modernize an organization's IT infrastructure by adopting new digital innovations, like cloud-based solutions, machine learning, and the interconnected network of

devices, known as the Internet of Things (IoT). These technologies can allow organizations to optimize their IT infrastructure and create more flexible and scalable systems. Cloud computing, for example, allows organizations to
store and access data and apps over the Internet instead of
relying on physical servers.

This can help organizations to reduce their hardware prices, improve their data security, and scale their IT infrastructure more quickly.

Artificial intelligence can also help businesses to modernize their IT infrastructure by automating routine tasks, such as data entry or customer service questions. This can free up employees to focus on higher-value tasks and improve the overall efficiency of the company. Similarly, the Internet of Things (IoT) can allow organizations to collect and analyze data from connected devices, such as sensors and smart machines, to gain insights into their operations and customers.

This can help organizations to optimize their processes, reduce downtime, and build new products and services.

Overall, digital transformation can help organizations to modernize their IT infrastructure by adopting new digital technologies that can improve their operations, reduce costs, and create new possibilities for growth.

- **It increases revenue with more relevant goods and services:** Revamp Digital transformation can indeed increase revenue by enabling companies to give more relevant products and services to their customers.

Through digital technologies, businesses can gather vast amounts of data about their customers, including their preferences, behaviors, and needs. This data can then be used to develop personalized goods and services that are tailored to individual customer needs.

For example, an online retailer can use customer data to recommend goods based on past purchases, search history, and preferences.

A healthcare provider can use data to offer personalized treatment plans and online services.

A bank can use data to offer customized financial goods and services based on a customer's spending and saving habits. By leveraging digital technologies to offer more relevant goods and services, businesses can improve customer satisfaction and loyalty, leading to increased revenue and profits. Additionally, digital transformation can also help companies streamline operations, reduce costs, and improve efficiency, further adding to revenue growth.

Chapter Four

Is digital transformation a good career?

Digital transformation is a rapidly emerging field with tremendous career possibilities. As firms increasingly embrace digital technology to better their business processes, the demand for employees with skills and knowledge in digital transformation is on the rise.

Digital transformation careers can range across numerous industries and activities, including IT, marketing, operations, finance, and more. Some prominent digital transformation job titles are digital transformation consultant, digital transformation manager, digital project manager, digital strategist, and chief digital officer.

However, like any career, success in digital transformation involves a combination of technical expertise, soft skills, and a commitment to continuously learn and adapt.

It also entails keeping up with the latest developments and innovations in the sector.

Overall, digital transformation can be a fulfilling career path for those who are passionate about technology, innovation, and making a beneficial impact on organizations and society.

Chapter Five

Does digital transformation needs coding?

Digital transformation is a broad word that refers to the integration of digital technology into all sectors of an organization, resulting in fundamental changes to how the business runs and delivers value to consumers.

While coding can

certainly be a beneficial ability to have during the digital transformation process, it is not always necessary.

Digital transformation can encompass a wide range of actions, including adopting new digital tools and systems, developing new processes and workflows, revamping consumer experiences, and employing data analytics to make better decisions.

While some of these activities may require coding expertise, many others do not.

For example, a corporation might undergo a digital transformation by deploying a new customer relationship management (CRM) system that does not require any coding to set up and use. Alternatively, a corporation might focus on reinventing its customer experience by doing user research, developing new interfaces, and testing new procedures without having any technical abilities.

That being said, having a rudimentary understanding of coding can surely be advantageous throughout a digital transformation.

It can help users to understand how digital tools and systems work and can enable them to

make more educated decisions about which technologies to adopt and how to utilize them successfully. However,
it is not a precondition for digital transformation.

Chapter Six

Which expertise is required for digital transformation?

The term **"digital transformation"** refers to a broad range of projects and tools that use digital technologies to improve business processes and addvalue. For digital transformation initiatives to be effective, several skills are essential. The following are some essential abilities:

- **Foundational knowledge of digital technologies,** such as cloud computing, data analytics, artificial intelligence, machine learning, and the Internet of Things, is crucial.

People with digital literacy are better able to understand and interact with the digital world.

- **Strategic Approach:** Digital transformation calls for a strategic approach that connects organizational objectives with technology initiatives. Effective strategic thinking entails analyzing the present situation, imagining the ideal future situation, and developing a plan to close the gap while taking the competitive environment, market trends, and the customer wants into account.

- **Change management:** Considerable Organizational changes are frequently a part of digital transformation.

The capacity to manage and drive change is essential for implementation success. Effective communication, stakeholder involvement, developing an innovative culture, and getting through opposition to change are all skills in the field of change management.

- **Data analysis:** Businesses produce enormous volumes of data, making it crucial to be able to examine it and draw conclusions from it.

Organizations can use data analysis skills, such as data mining, data visualization, and statistical analysis, to make data-driven decisions, spot patterns, and get insightful business knowledge.

- **Collaboration and cross-functional skills:** Digital transformation projects frequently include collaboration between different teams and departments. Individuals may work together, dismantle organizational silos, share knowledge, and use various viewpoints to spur innovation and accomplish shared objectives with the help of effective collaboration and cross-functional abilities.

- **Digital security and privacy have become more important as society relies more on digital technologies.** For the protection of data, the reduction of cyber risks, and compliance, it is crucial to comprehend the fundamentals of digital security, risk management, and privacy rules.

- **Continuous Learning and Adaptability:** People must embrace lifetime learning and maintain their adaptability because the digital landscape is constantly changing.

People may stay relevant and lead effective digital transformation initiatives by staying up to date with technical developments, industry trends, and the acquisition of new skills.

It's significant to highlight that depending on the sector, size, and objectives of the firm, different talents may be necessary for digital transformation. But the aforementioned abilities offer a base for negotiating the challenges of digital change.

Chapter Seven

What are the 3 R's of digital transformation?

The three pillars of digital transformation are what?

The following is a common description of the 3 R's of digital transformation:

- **Reimagine**: This is the process of using digital technologies to reimagine or rethink current company processes, strategies, and models.

It entails questioning established practices and investigating cutting-edge uses of digital technologies and platforms to boost growth, improve consumer experiences, and increase operational effectiveness.

- **Restructure**: This requires changing the organization's structure to meet the demands of digital transformation.

It entails rearranging teams, roles, and duties to make room for fresh digital projects. Along with building agile and collaborative processes, the restructuring calls for dismantling silos and promoting a culture of ongoing learning and adaptation.

- **Reinvent**: Reinvention entails embracing an innovative and improving culture.

It involves experimenting with cutting-edge technologies to develop new business models and value propositions, such like artificial intelligence (AI), machine learning (ML), blockchain, or the Internet of Things (IoT). To remain successful in the digital era, reinventing also entails responding to shifting client wants and market conditions.

It's important to keep in mind that alternative frameworks could exist in addition to the 3 R's of digital transformation, depending on the source.

To thrive in the digital age, the organization must be reimagined, restructured, and reinvented.

Chapter Eight

What are the essential skills for digital transformation?

Digital transformation encompasses a comprehensive range of activities and technologies aimed at leveraging digital capabilities to enhance business processes, customer experiences, and overall organizational performance. While the specific skills necessary for digital transformation may vary depending on the industry and context, several core skills are generally essential for successful digital transformation initiatives. These abilities include:

- **Digital literacy:** A fundamental understanding of digital technologies, their applications, and their potential impact on business operations is crucial. This includes knowledge of fundamental computer skills, software applications, data analytics, cloud computing, and emerging technologies.

- **Strategic thinking:** The ability to think strategically and envision how digital technologies can be used to drive innovation, enhance operational efficiency, and create new business opportunities. This involves identifying the organization's goals, aligning digital initiatives with business objectives, and devising a clear roadmap for digital transformation.

- **Leadership and change management:** Digital transformation often necessitates significant organizational change. Effective leaders are needed to oversee the transformation process, communicate the vision, and inspire and motivate employees.

Change management skills, such as stakeholder engagement, communication, and conflict resolution, are essential for promoting adoption and overcoming resistance to change.

- **Data analysis and interpretation:** Digital transformation relies heavily on data-driven decision-making. Proficiency in data analysis and interpretation enables organizations to extricate insights, identify trends, and make informed strategic choices. Skills in data visualization, statistical analysis, and data narrative are valuable for effectively communicating data-driven insights to stakeholders.

- **Collaboration and cross-functional teamwork:** Digital transformation initiatives typically involve multiple departments and stakeholders. The ability to collaborate across functions, break down silos, and cultivate teamwork is crucial. This includes skills in effective communication, negotiation, and relationship building to facilitate collaboration and receive buy-in from diverse stakeholders.

- **Agile and adaptable mindset:** Digital transformation initiatives often operate in a swiftly evolving and unpredictable environment. An agile and adaptable mindset allows organizations to respond quickly to changing market dynamics, adopt new technologies, and perpetually iterate and improve digital solutions. This includes embracing experimentation, learning from failures, and being receptive to new ideas and approaches.

- **Cybersecurity awareness:** As organizations incorporate digital

  technologies, the need for robust cybersecurity measures becomes paramount. A basic understanding of cybersecurity principles, risk management, and privacy regulations is essential to safeguard digital assets, and customer data, and ensure compliance.

- **Customer-centricity:** Digital transformation is ultimately driven by the aim of delivering enhanced customer experiences. Skills in customer research, design thinking, and user experience (UX) design are crucial for understanding customer requirements, designing intuitive digital interfaces, and creating customer-centric solutions.

- **Continuous learning:** Digital transformation is an ongoing process, and the digital landscape is continuously evolving. Cultivating a culture of continuous learning is critical to remain updated with the latest trends, technologies, and best practices. This involves being proactive in seeking new knowledge, attending relevant training programs, and remaining connected with

industry networks and communities.

By developing and nurturing these core skills, organizations can better navigate the complexities of digital transformation and leverage digital technologies to drive innovation, enhance competitiveness, and achieve long-term success.

www.ingramcontent.com/pod-product-compliance
Lightning Source LLC
Chambersburg PA
CBHW030511220526
45464CB00006B/2755